Math 'a' Stick

PUFFIN BOOKS

An imprint of Penguin Random House

PUFFIN BOOKS

USA | Canada | UK | Ireland | Australia
New Zealand | India | South Africa | China | Singapore

Puffin Books is part of the Penguin Random House group of companies
whose addresses can be found at global.penguinrandomhouse.com

Published by Penguin Random House India Pvt. Ltd
4th Floor, Capital Tower 1, MG Road,
Gurugram 122 002, Haryana, India

First published in Puffin Books by Penguin Random House India 2018

Text, design and illustrations copyright © Quadrum Solutions Pvt. Ltd 2018
Series copyright © Penguin Random House India 2018

ISBN 9780143444862

Design and layout by Quadrum Solutions Pvt. Ltd

Printed at Repro India Limited

www.penguin.co.in

Dear Moms and Dads,

In the twenty-first century, logic skills have become an intrinsic part of the skills required for children to grow into confident adults. To be ready to absorb more complex mathematical concepts later in life, maths readiness has assumed greater importance than ever before. That is why it has become ever so important to prep children while they are young and eager to learn.

The **Fun with Maths** series seeks to do just that—let children loose on the joy of applying logic and building mathematical skills as they go.

We created these books for children to explore the wonders of mathematics. Here's a peek into what they will learn (without even knowing they have learnt it):

1 Mathematical operations such as addition, subtraction, division and multiplication

2 Logical reasoning and spatial awareness

3 Patterns, symmetry and geometry

4 Application of mathematics in everyday life

It's been great creating this series with my highly charged Quadrum team: maths experts Krupa Shah and Madhavi Nathan, who spent hours crafting each page; Himani, who designed every page into a visual treat; Dinesh, who provided creative guidance; Kushal, who painstakingly laid out every number and sign; Bishnupriya and Ruby, who read and re-read every word; and Kunjli, who was the conscience of the entire series. And, of course, the Puffin team, Sohini and Mriga, who added value at every step. When you have a great team, you're bound to have a great book.

Thank you, guys!

Sonia Mehta

PS: We'd love your feedback, so do write in to us at

funlearningbooks@quadrumltd.com

Hello Kids

Here's your chance to throw that pencil and eraser away. Pull out those matchsticks, ice-cream sticks and toothpicks, and gather some paper and glue, and we are ready for some fun maths time.

Math-a-Stick is a fun way to explore various maths concepts. Play with the sticks, and move them around till you find the answer.

Remember to keep all the required essentials ready before you start the activity so that you don't have to stop midway through a puzzle.

Some activities allow you to work in the book itself, while others require you to solve the puzzles outside the book.

Math-o-Bot Challenge

You will see Math-o-Bot, the maths genius, popping up from time to time with exciting challenges so you can test how much you know. Give yourself a pat on the back when you complete them.

Safety Tip

Remember to leave the matchbox with your parents and use only the matchsticks. Or even better, ask them to give you only used matchsticks so that we stay and play safe!

And, of course, ask them for help when you can't figure out what to do next!

Have loads of Math-a-Stick fun!

Smallest and Largest

Which is the smallest two-digit number you can create using 11 matchsticks? Which is the largest two-digit number you can create using 11 matchsticks?

Place your answer here.

Smallest

Largest

Which Is Bigger?

Observe the statement given below. It is incorrect.

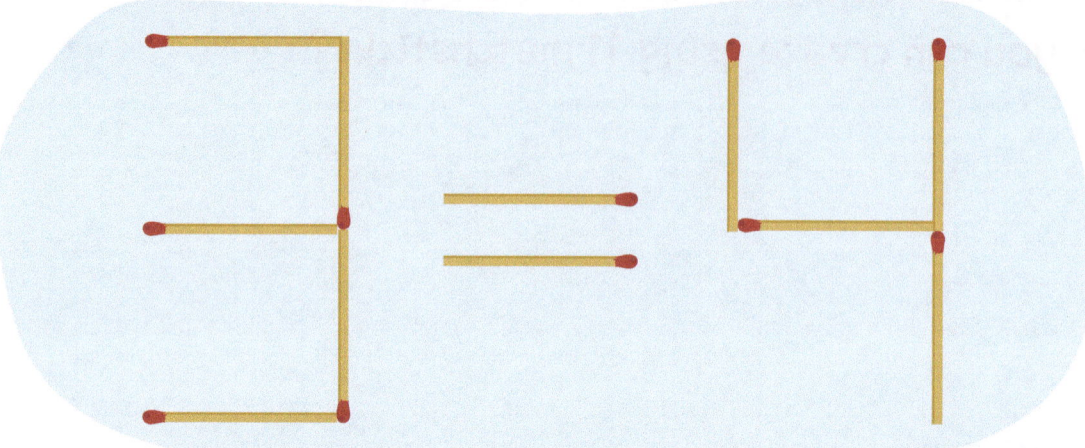

Can you move just 2 matchsticks so that this statement can be corrected?

Compare Them

Focus on changing the number, not the sign.

Here are some numbers. Can you make the statement true by moving only 2 matchsticks?

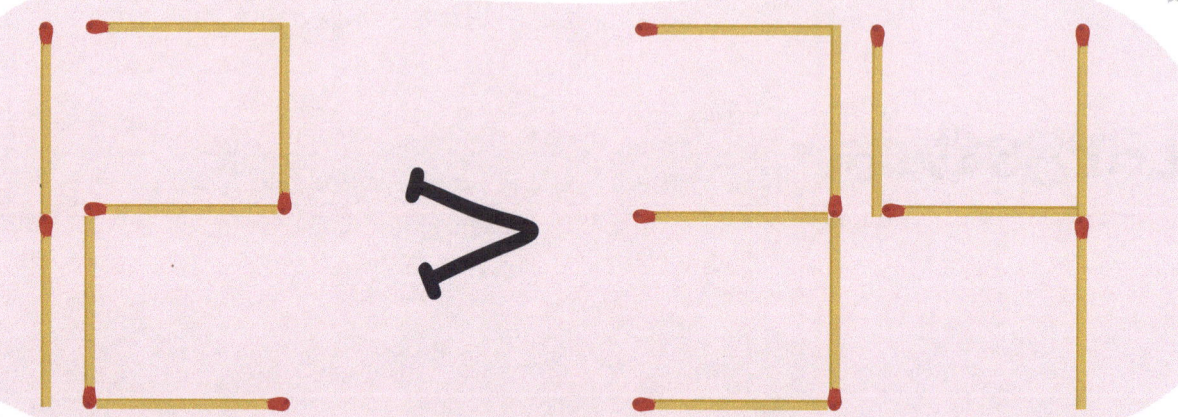

triangle tangle

Here are triangles made up with 9 matchsticks. Can you remove 3 matchsticks so that you are left with only 1 triangle?

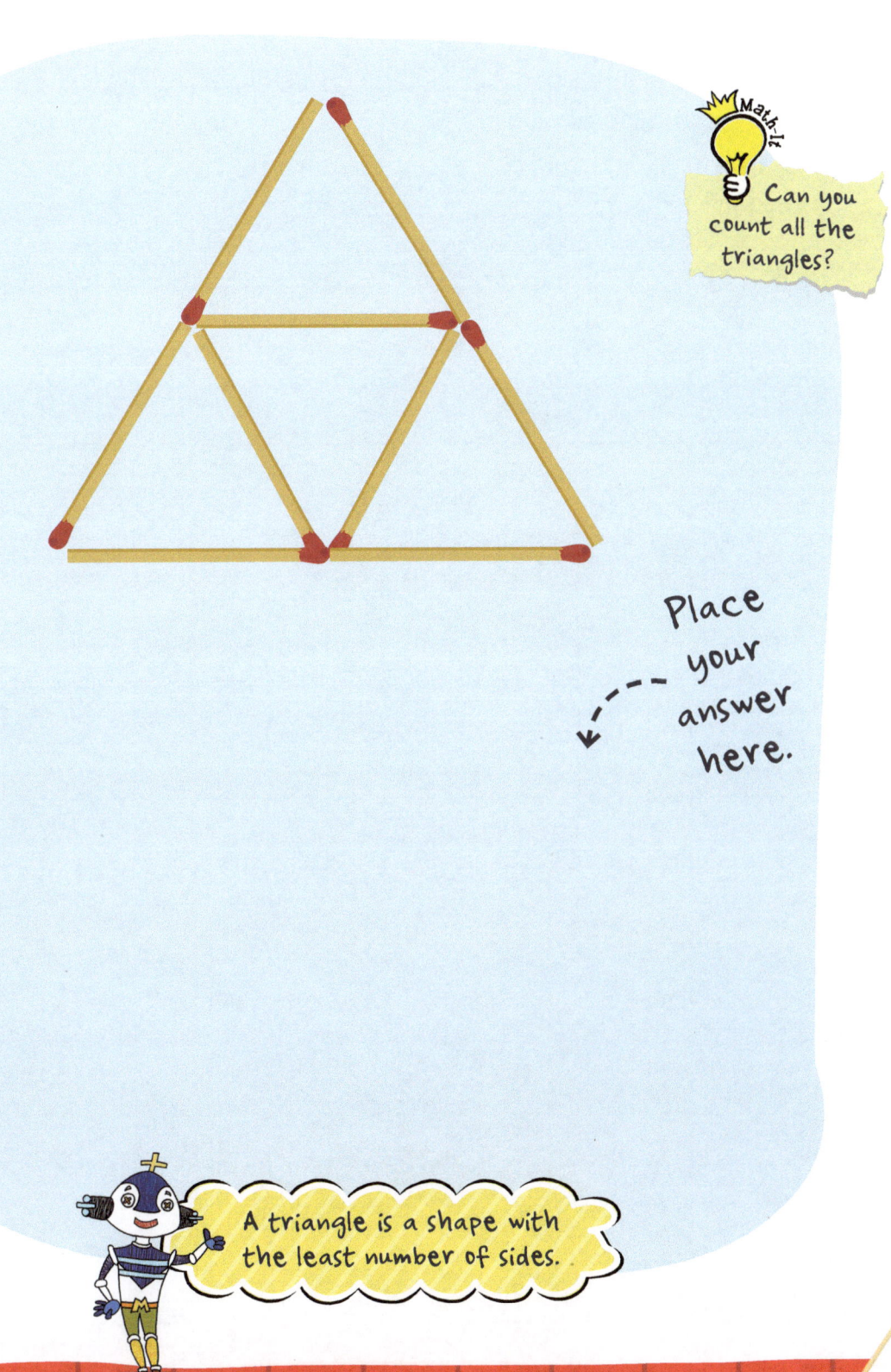

Math-It

Can you count all the triangles?

Place your answer here.

A triangle is a shape with the least number of sides.

Tri-angled

Use 18 toothpicks to create 13 triangles. You can arrange the toothpicks in any manner you like.

All triangles do not have to be of the same size.

← Place your answer here.

Seven Up, Seven Down

The addition statement below can be corrected by moving just 1 matchstick. Which one will you move?

Remember the rules of addition.

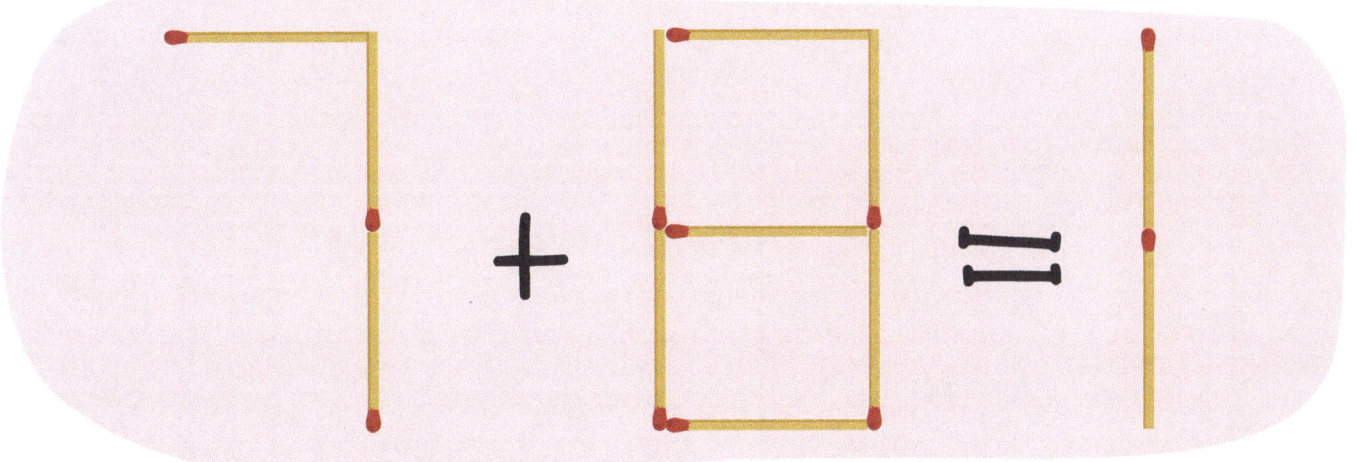

Plus Fuss

There is something wrong with the addition statement below. Can you correct the statement by using 4 more matchsticks?

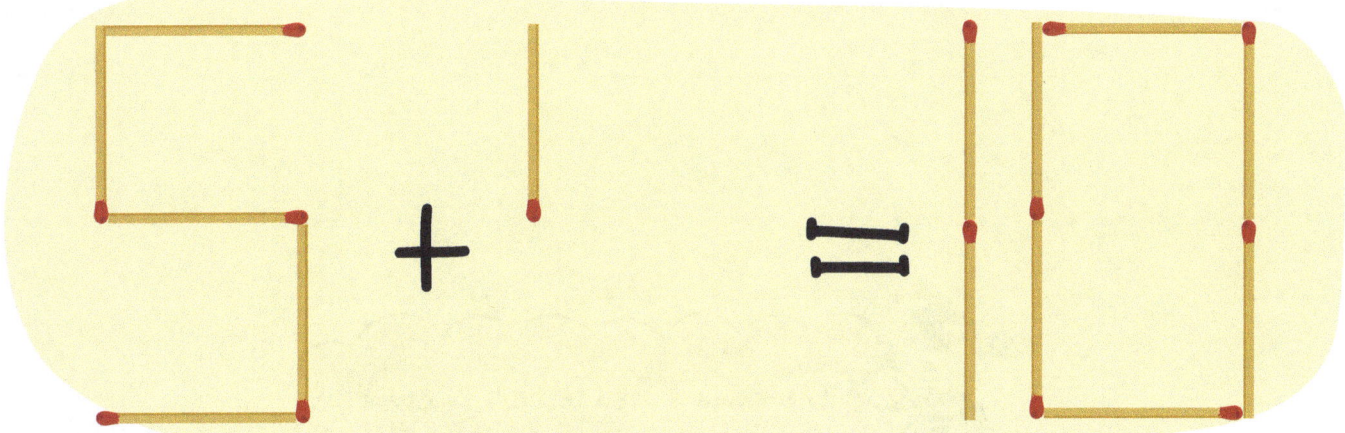

TWO PLUS TWO

We have 2 plus 2 here. Can you make 4 using only 3 ice-cream sticks?

You cannot write four like this 4.

← Place your answer here.

The Romans used letters to count.

Top Ten

You have 20 matchsticks. You take away 5 and are left with 10. How can you make this happen?

Math-It

Think of different ways in which you can write 10.

Place your answer here.

The number 10 is the base of our number system.

Fun with Seven

The statement below is absolutely correct. Can you move just 1 matchstick and still ensure that this statement is correct?

Fix the Six

7 – 0 is not 6. Then what is it? Can you move only 2 matchsticks to make this statement correct?

Math-it

Focus on changing the sum, not the answer.

Math-o-Bot's Number Challenge

A

Add the following numbers:

```
  65
+  4
------
```

```
  87
+  8
------
```

```
  30
+ 45
------
```

B

Can you arrange the following numbers in the ascending order?

78, 53, 74, 69, 27

_____

C

Can you arrange the following numbers in the descending order?

63, 76, 54, 93, 87

_____

D

Use < , > or = sign in the sums given below. You can use each sign only once.

45 [ ] 54

78 [ ] 71

81 [ ] 81

Toothpick Squares

Create 9 squares by using 14 toothpicks. You can arrange the toothpicks in any manner you like.

The squares will not be equal in size.

Place your answer here.

Six by six

We have a hexagon here. Can you add 6 ice-cream sticks to make 6 triangles?

Place your answer here.

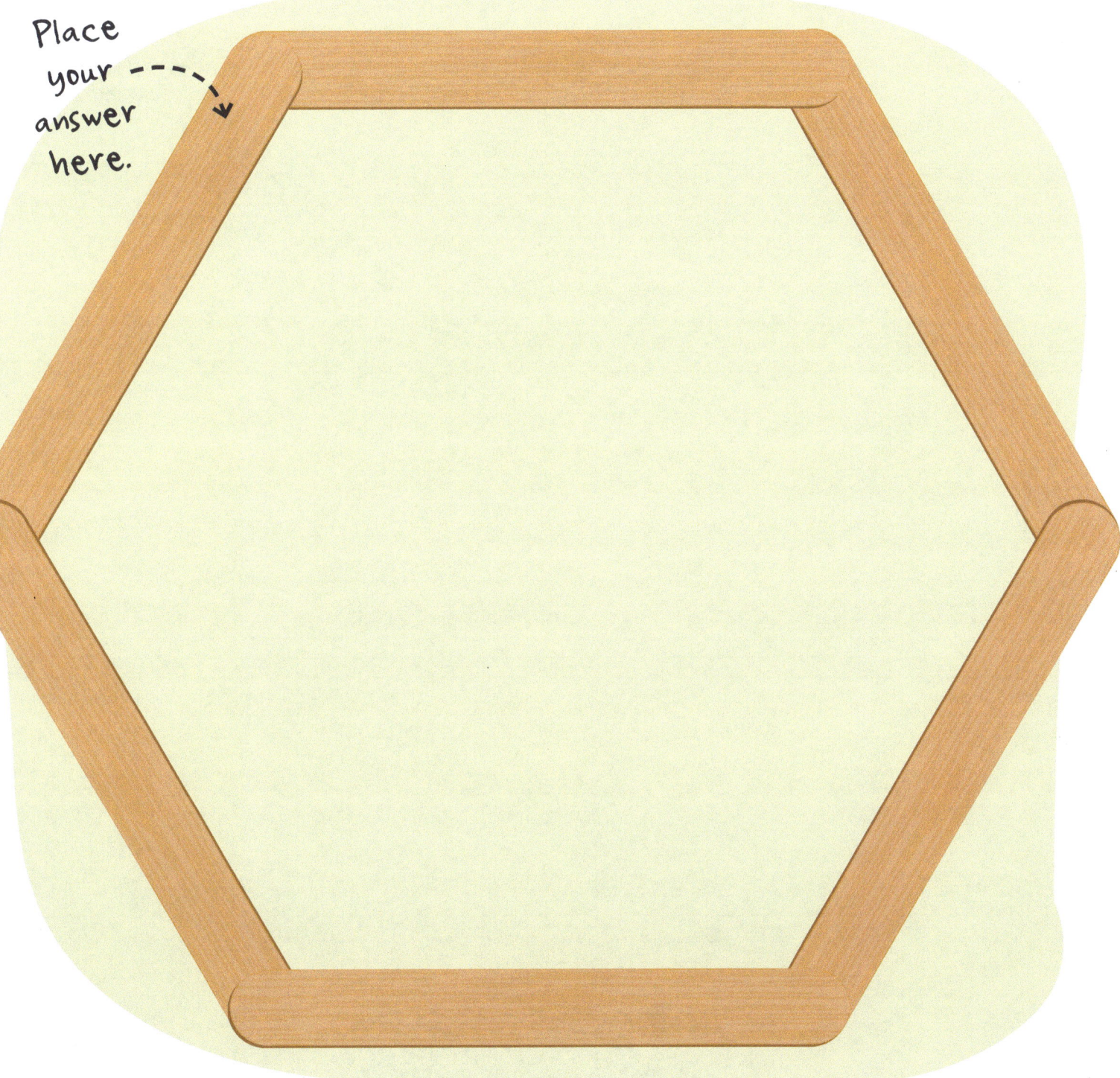

Make Ten

How can you use two dozen matchsticks to make 10 squares?

Math-le

12 makes a dozen.

Place your answer here.

10 is the smallest two-digit number.

Triangle Time

Here is a triangle made by using 18 matchsticks. Can you take away 4 matchsticks, so that you are left with 6 triangles? You can simply cross the matchsticks out.

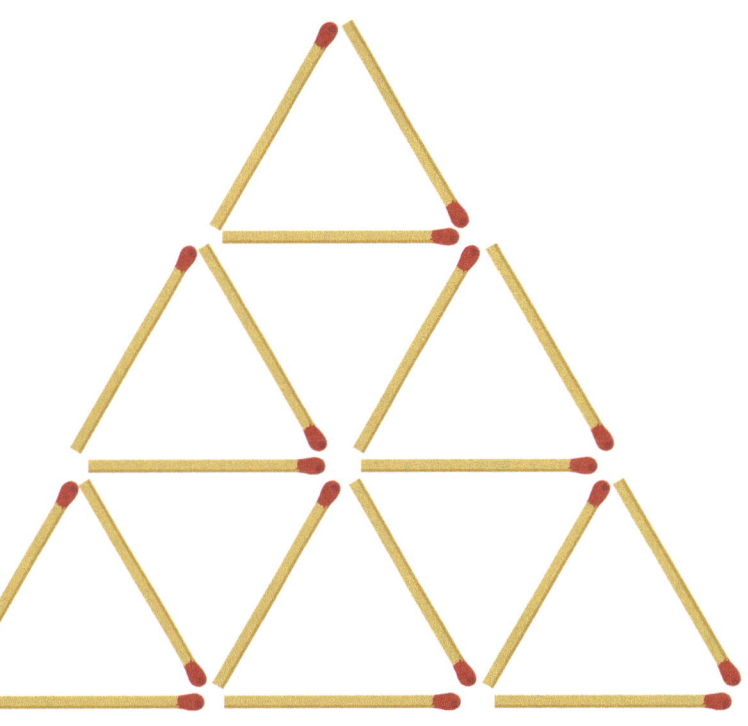

Two by Two

This grid is made up of 24 matchsticks. Can you take away 4 matchsticks to make only 9 squares? You can simply cross the matchsticks out.

A square is also a rectangle with equal sides.

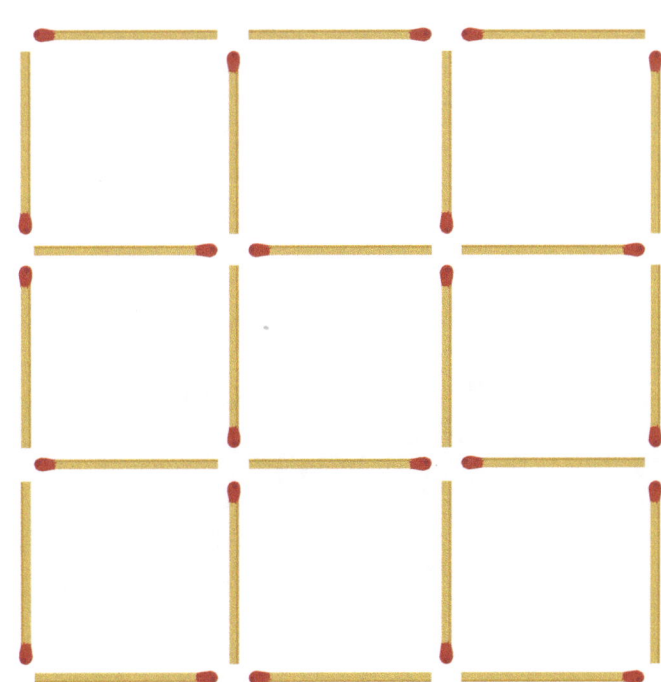

Square It up

Here is a square made with 12 matchsticks. Can you add 6 matchsticks to make 3 squares?

You can solve this in 4 ways. There is one shown in the answer sheet.

Place your answer here.

The square is the only regular quadrilateral.

Four by Six

Here are 5 squares. Can you form 6 squares by moving just 4 matchsticks?

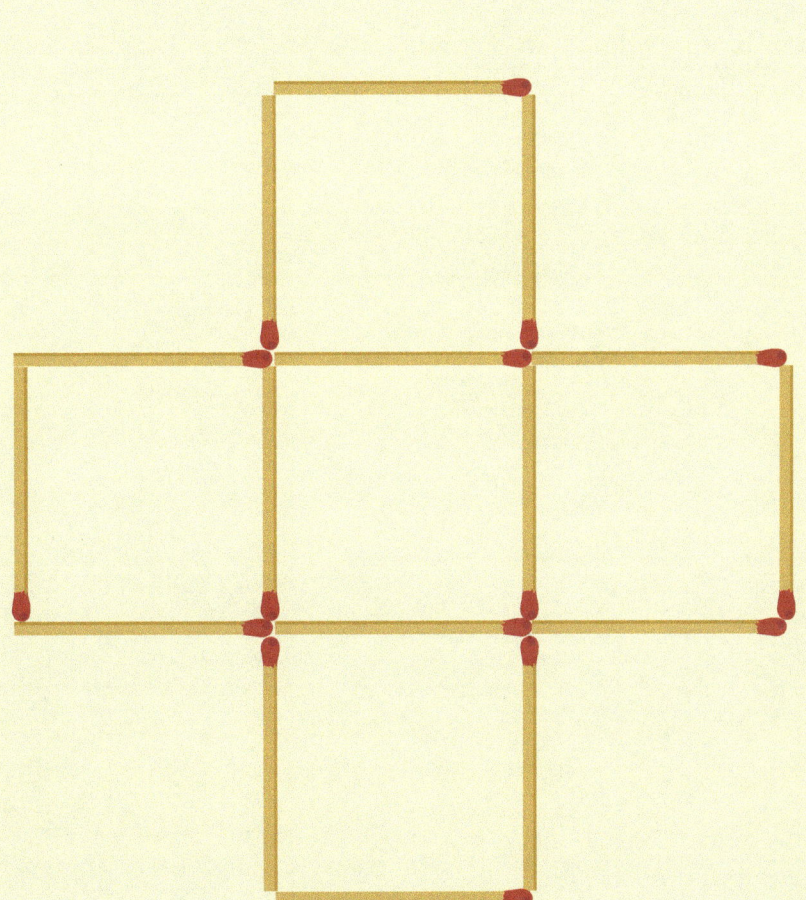

Fair and Square

Take 18 matchsticks. Can you arrange them in a way that they create 6 squares of the same size?

Remember not to count the big square.

Place your answer here.

6 is the smallest perfect number.

Shape up

You have been practising shapes. Can you transform the hexagon below into a parallelogram? You have to move 4 matchsticks to make a parallelogram.

A parallelogram is a quadrilateral with opposite sides parallel.

Cube It

We have a cube made up of 12 matchsticks and some glue. Can you create the same and count the number of squares you have? You can also use some clay to hold the sticks together.

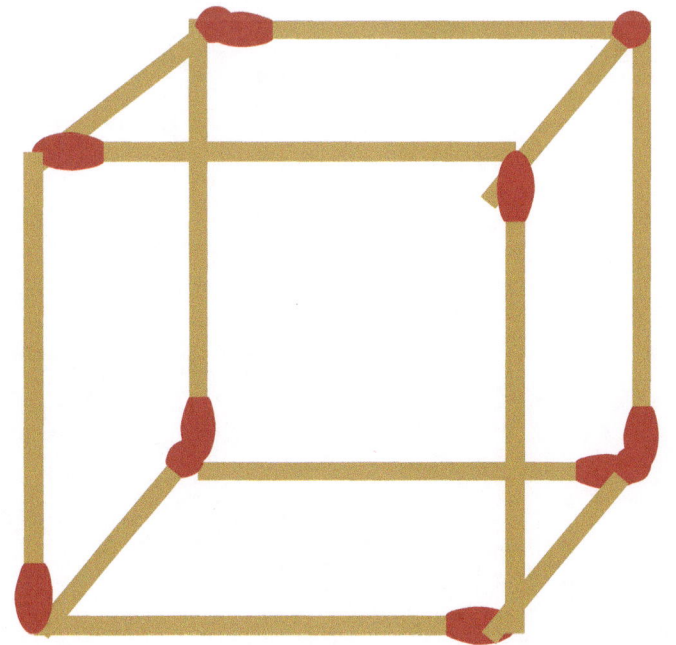

High Five

Can you make 5 triangles using 5 ice-cream sticks?

Place your answer here. →

Careful! Don't break the sticks.

A 5-point star is a decagon, that is, it has 10 sides.

Fine Nine

Here are 6 matchsticks. Can you add 5 more and make 9?

Place your answer here.

3 squared is 9.

Numero Uno

There are many ways to get to a number. Can you use 6 matchsticks and complete the statement below? You have to fill up the 3 blanks.

Think of the different number operations you can use.

Place your answer here.

$$\underline{\quad\quad} \quad \underline{\quad\quad} \quad \underline{\quad\quad} \quad = \; |$$

1 is neither a prime nor a composite number.

Dozen

Can you correct the below statement by moving only 2 matchsticks? Ensure that the answer is 12.

$$3 + 4 = 12$$

Three Times

Here is a correct multiplication statement. Can you keep it a correct multiplication statement by removing 6 matchsticks?

$$3 \times 8 = 24$$

Cake Cutting

Here is a cake. Use 3 ice-cream sticks to cut the cake in a way that you get 7 pieces.

Place the ice-cream sticks on this cake.

Math-It
The pieces do not have to be of the same size.

Math-o-Bot's Number Challenge

A

Multiply the following numbers:

5 x 8

3 x 6

5 x 7

10 x 4

2 x 8

B

Can you match the following objects to their shadows?

 •

 •

 •

 •

 •

C

You have 12 pencils. How many will you have in a group if you make 3 equal groups?

Art Work

Here is a part of an incomplete design. Use some matchsticks to finish the remaining three parts to get a perfectly symmetrical design.

Keep in mind the lines of symmetry.

Place your answer here.

A shape that is not symmetrical is called asymmetrical.

One Line

Use 10 matchsticks to create a design of your choice that has ONLY one line of symmetry.

Here is my design.

Place your answer here.

Line up

Use up to 8 ice-cream sticks to create a design of your choice that has 2 or more lines of symmetry.

Here is my design.

Place your answer here.

Five Houses

Here is a house made up of 6 matchsticks. Can you arrange 23 matchsticks in a way that you make 5 similar houses?

Place your answer here.

The houses can share walls as well as roofs and can even be upside down.

There are 5 rings in the Olympic symbol.

Square to Pair

Here is a big square. Can you add 10 matchsticks to divide it into 2 equal parts?

Both parts must be the same in shape, size and form.

2 is the smallest prime number.

Place your answer here.

Worming Away

10 worms are going to the right as they follow the leader. Can you re-arrange only 3 toothpicks in a way that it seems that the worms are now going to the left but the pattern remains the same?

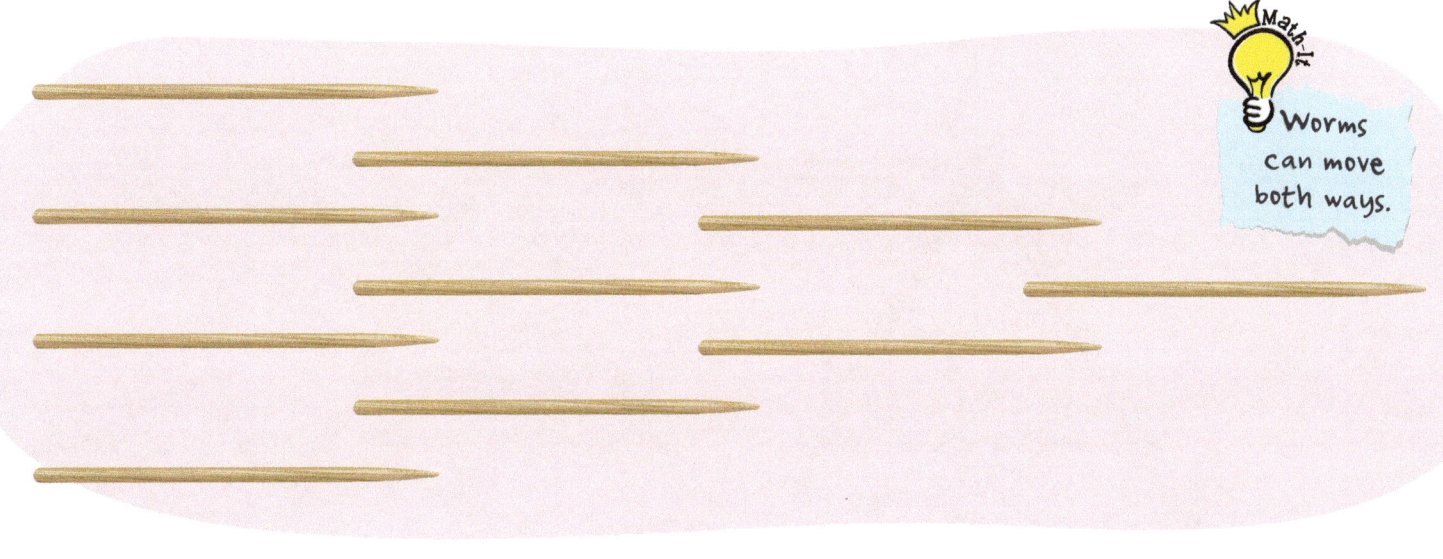

Worms can move both ways.

Two Glasses

Here are 2 dots and 2 glasses. Can you move only 3 matchsticks so that the dots are inside the glasses? You cannot move the dots.

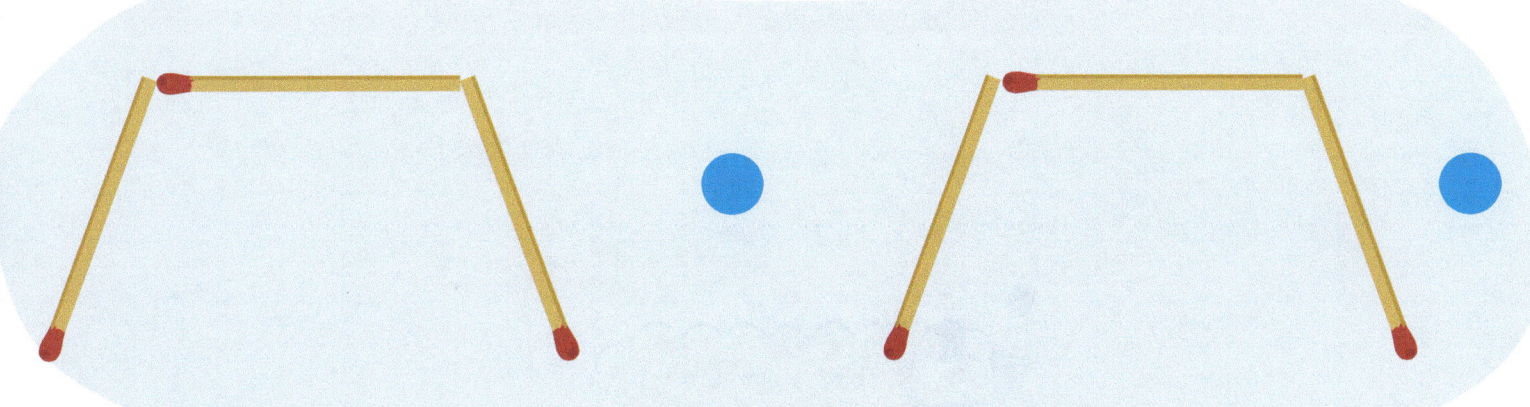

Six to Three

Here is a hexagon. Can you make 3 triangles by moving only 4 toothpicks?

Honeycombs have hexagons too.

Equal Triangle

Here is an equal triangle. Use 3 toothpicks to divide this triangle into 3 equal parts. You can paste them here.

Math-It

The shape and size of all parts have to be the same.

Place your answer here.

A triangle where all sides and angles are equal is called an equilateral triangle.

Shape Tally

Look at the number of tally marks against each shape. Put a tick if the answer is correct and a cross if it is wrong.

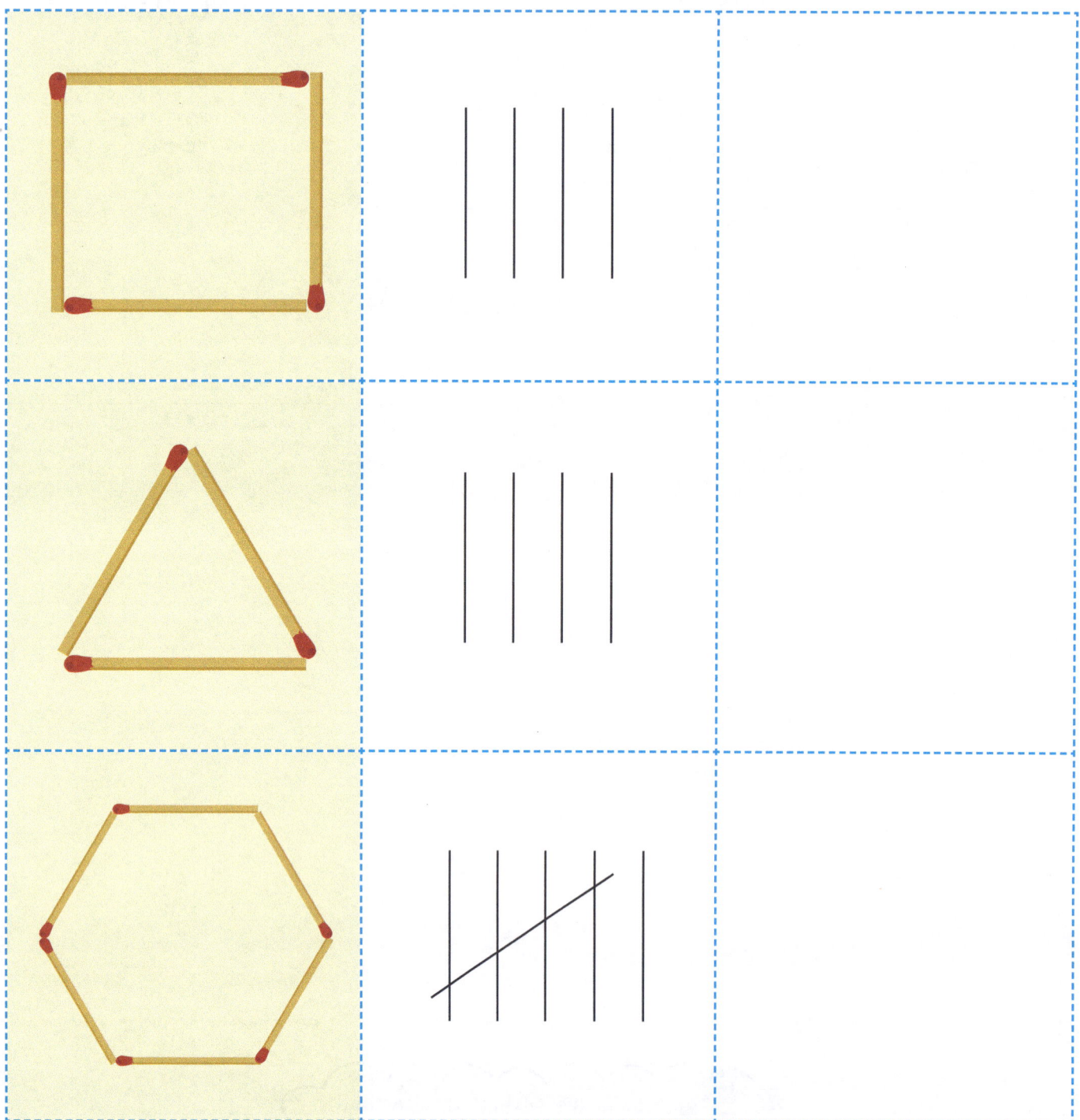

Measure up

Here are a rectangle and a triangle. Measure the perimeter of the rectangle using matchsticks and the triangle using ice-cream sticks. How many matchsticks and ice-cream sticks will you need?

Matchsticks

Ice-cream sticks

Perimeter is the sum of the sides of a shape.

Tally Away

Look at the letters below and show the tally marks for each.

Tally marks are always in groups of 5 ⵑⵑ.

Twin Triangles

Here are 4 triangles. Can you make only 2 triangles by moving just 4 matchsticks?

Both triangles have to be of the same size.

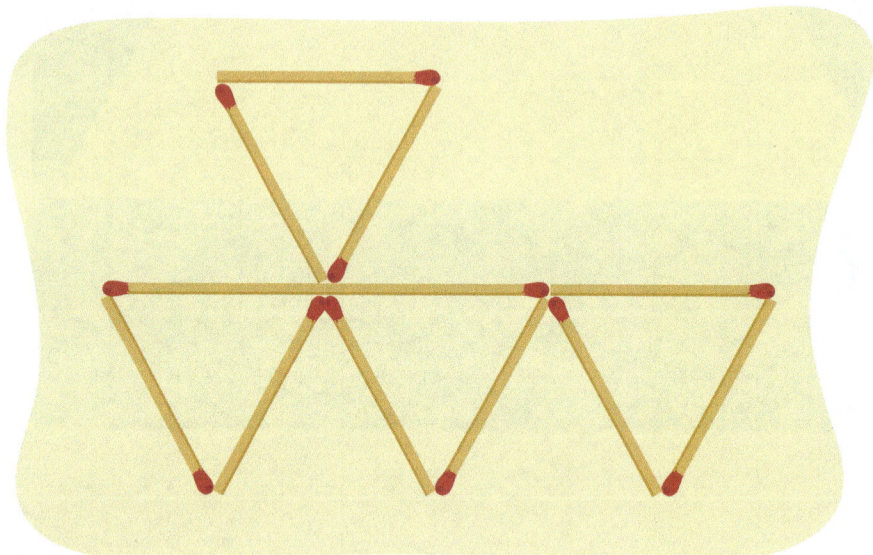

Math-o-Bot's Number Challenge

This chart shows us how much water each child drinks in a day. Study it carefully and answer the questions.

 = 1 glass of water

Tina									
Raj								
Ali								
Sonia									
Rita								
Mina								
Jack								

- Who drinks the most water in a day? _____

- How much water does Ali drink in a day? _____

- Which 2 children drink the same amount of water? _____

- Who drinks the least water in a day? _____

- Who drinks 3 glasses of water in a day? _____

Small Triangles

Here, 10 matchsticks have been used to make 8 small triangles. Can you arrange 10 matchsticks on the grid to make 14 small triangles?

Place your answer here.

10 years make a decade.

Arrowheads

12 arrows have been placed in the grid below. Do you think you can place 12 more arrows in a way that none of the arrowheads meet?

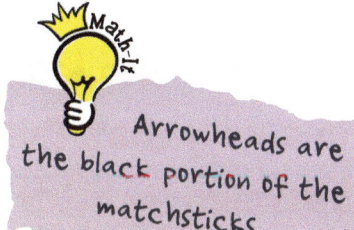

Arrowheads are the black portion of the matchsticks.

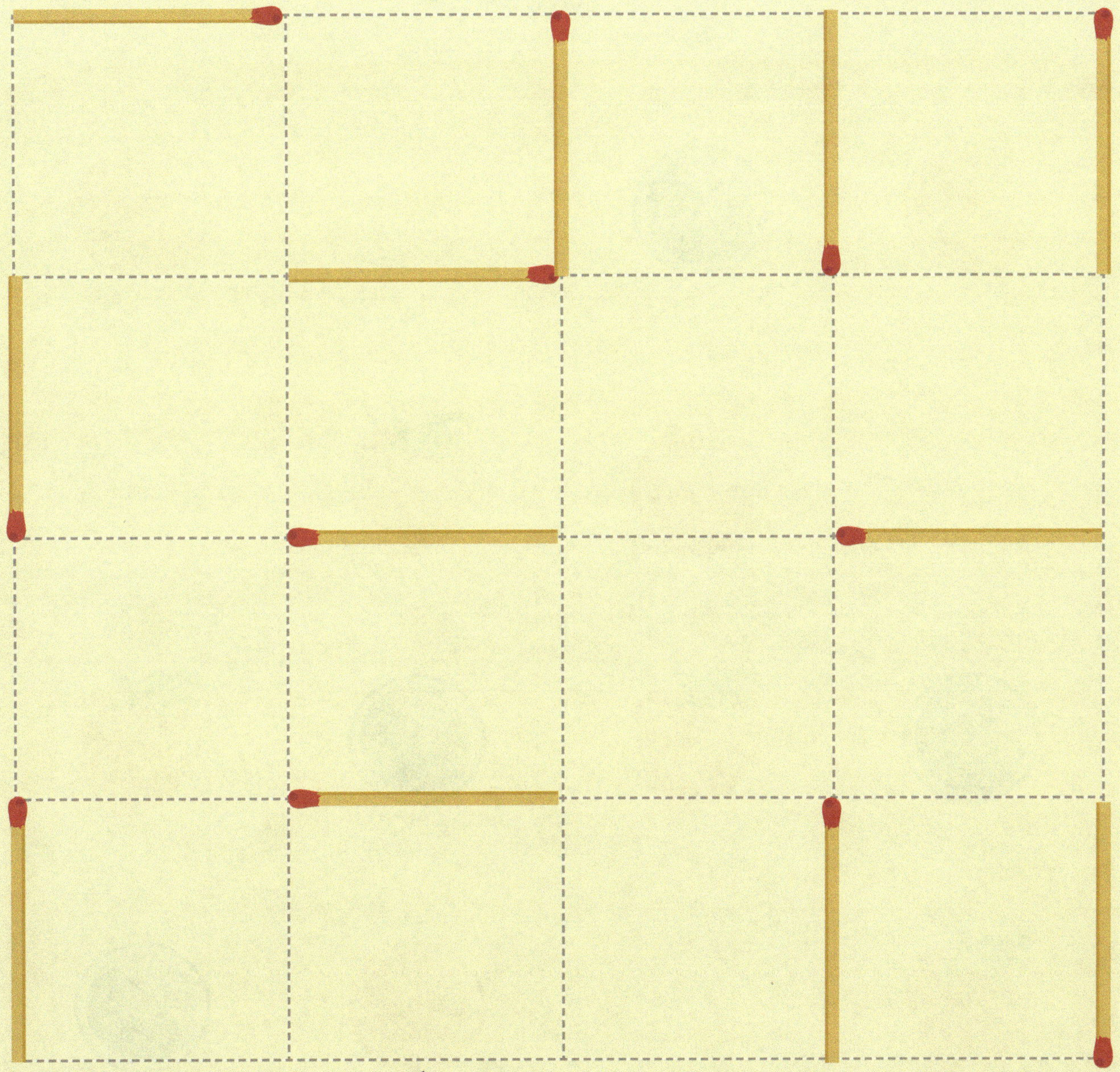

Place your answer here.

Fruit Cookie

This fruit cookie has 4 strawberries, 4 cherries and 4 grapes. Can you cut the cookie in a way that the cookie is equally divided between 4 children?

Place your answer here.

Math-It

Each child must get a piece of each fruit and the piece of the cookie must be of the same size and shape.

Equal to Five

Here are 9 equal squares. Take away 6 matchsticks to make 5 equal squares.

Multiples of 5 always have 5 or 0 in the ones place.

Zero Hero

You have 26 matchsticks. You take away 5 and are left with O. How do you think that happened? Show your answer in the space below.

Place your answer here.

Four by Four

You will need 4 whole matchsticks and 4 half matchsticks. Can you create 3 squares with these matchsticks?

Place your answer here.

Diamonds

Here is a diamond. Can you add 10 matchsticks to it to make 5 diamonds?

Place your answer here.

4 Square

Here are 9 equal squares. Can you remove 10 matchsticks so that only 4 squares are remaining?

Math-It

All squares must be equal.

Answers

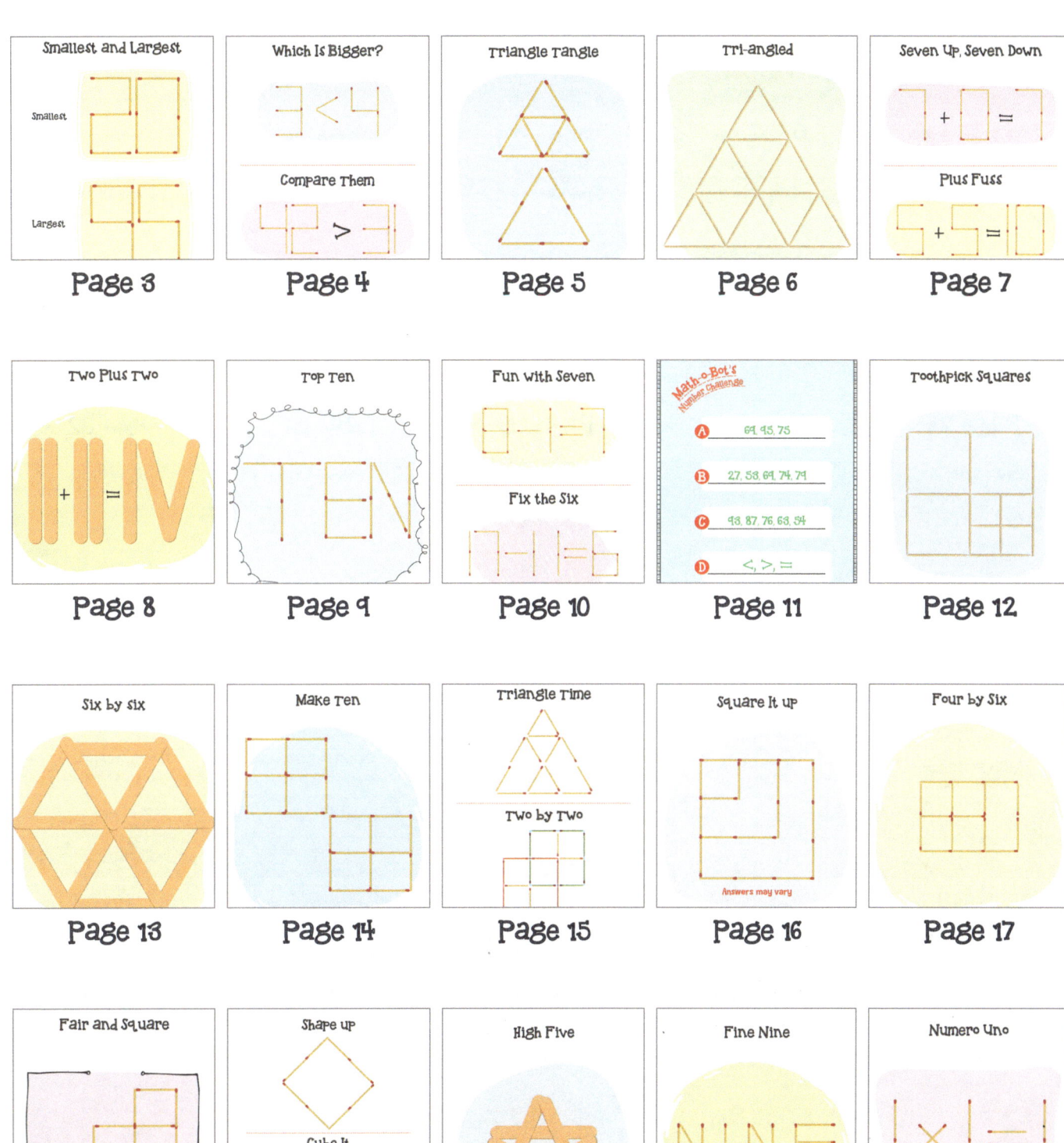

Smallest and Largest

Smallest

Largest

Page 3

Which Is Bigger?

3 < 4

Compare Them

4 2 > 3

Page 4

Triangle Tangle

Page 5

Tri-angled

Page 6

Seven Up, Seven Down

+ =

Plus Fuss

5 + 5 = 10

Page 7

Two Plus Two

III + I = IV

Page 8

Top Ten

TEN

Page 9

Fun with Seven

8 - 1 = 7

Fix the Six

7 - 1 = 6

Page 10

Math-o-Bot's
Number Challenge

A   69, 45, 75

B   27, 58, 69, 74, 79

C   93, 87, 76, 63, 54

D   <, >, =

Page 11

Toothpick Squares

Page 12

Six by Six

Page 13

Make Ten

Page 14

Triangle Time

Two by Two

Page 15

Square It Up

Answers may vary

Page 16

Four by Six

Page 17

Fair and Square

Page 18

Shape Up

Cube It

There are 6 squares.

Page 19

High Five

Page 20

Fine Nine

NINE

Page 21

Numero Uno

| × | = |

Page 22

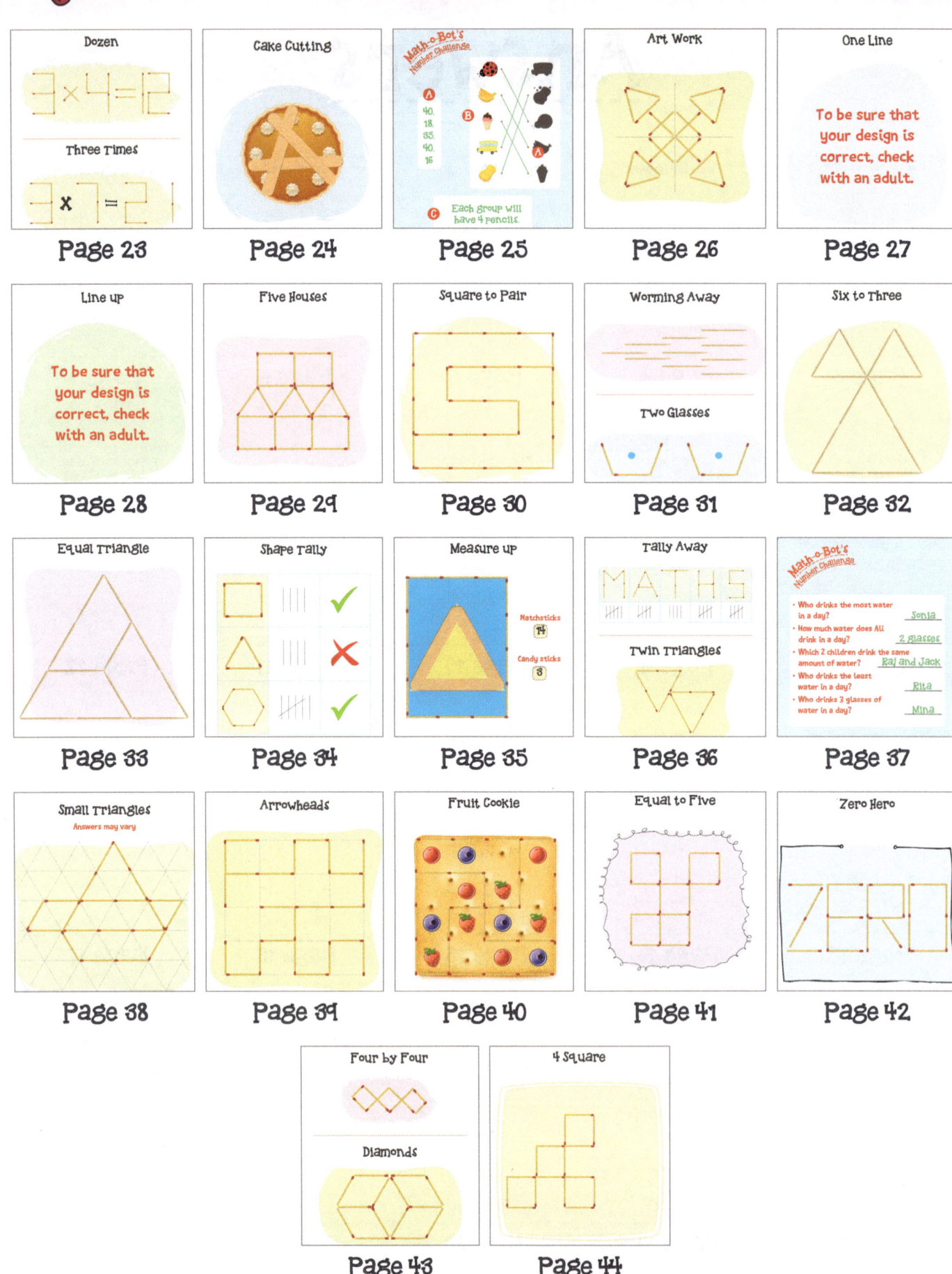

Dozen

Three Times

Page 23

Cake Cutting

Page 24

Math-o-Bot's Number Challenge

A
40,
18,
35,
40,
16

B

C   Each group will have 4 pencils.

Page 25

Art Work

Page 26

One Line

To be sure that your design is correct, check with an adult.

Page 27

Line up

To be sure that your design is correct, check with an adult.

Page 28

Five Houses

Page 29

Square to Pair

Page 30

Worming Away

Two Glasses

Page 31

Six to Three

Page 32

Equal Triangle

Page 33

Shape Tally

✓
✗
✓

Page 34

Measure up

Matchsticks 14

Candy sticks 3

Page 35

Tally Away

MATHS

Twin Triangles

Page 36

Math-o-Bot's Number Challenge

• Who drinks the most water in a day?   Sonia
• How much water does Ali drink in a day?   2 glasses
• Which 2 children drink the same amount of water?   Raj and Jack
• Who drinks the least water in a day?   Rita
• Who drinks 3 glasses of water in a day?   Mina

Page 37

Small Triangles

Answers may vary

Page 38

Arrowheads

Page 39

Fruit Cookie

Page 40

Equal to Five

Page 41

Zero Hero

Page 42

Four by Four

Diamonds

Page 43

4 Square

Page 44

46